Discovering DNA

This course was written by
Naturally Curious Expert
Jennifer Burbank

*Jennifer is a biologist who is curious about the DNA
instructions to make living things.*

Printed by CreateSpace

ISBN 978-1-942403-03-6

www.benaturallycurious.com

Many activities in this book make use of printed materials. If you prefer not to cut them directly from this book, please visit the URL listed below and enter the code for a supplemental PDF containing all printable materials.

URL: www.benaturallycurious.com/discovering-DNA-printables/

password: **helix**

Table of Contents

Required materials: Two thick pieces of licorice, toothpicks, mini marshmallows (four different colors) OR four different kinds of fruit, blender OR sealable plastic baggie, ½ cup of one of the following (fresh or frozen strawberries, peas, spinach, broccoli, or banana), measuring spoons, table salt, water, liquid dish detergent, clear plastic or glass cups, coffee filter or small strainer, ice-cold rubbing alcohol, popsicle stick or plastic coffee stirrer, scissors, 2 pieces of yarn or string (each about 5 feet long), tape, 9 friends or stuffed animals.

What is DNA?

Meet Desi! She is a **DNA** molecule. Maybe you have heard of DNA, but you aren't sure what it's all about. Desi and other DNA molecules just like her are found in every single cell of your body! DNA stands for a big phrase—*deoxyribonucleic acid*! Wow. We'll just stick with DNA in this story. Desi and her DNA friends have all of the instructions your cells need to build your body and make it work. Pretty neat, right? Today you get to travel into Desi's world to find out more about how she does her job.

Your DNA molecules contain all the information needed to make and work your body!

If we wanted to find Desi the DNA molecule, where would we look? Well, as we said, Desi and other DNA molecules are found in every cell of your body. Can you see them? You actually can't because they are very tiny. Take a look at your arm. The skin on your arm is made up of many, many skin cells. If we could look inside a skin cell, we would find a **NUCLEUS** at the center of it. A nucleus is a little structure inside a cell that controls what happens in the cell. This is where DNA hangs out! Desi and her DNA friends are there.

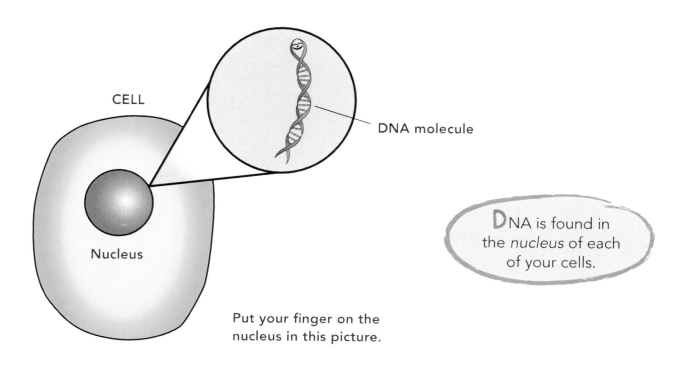

CELL

DNA molecule

Nucleus

DNA is found in the *nucleus* of each of your cells.

Put your finger on the nucleus in this picture.

DNA molecules are shaped like twisted ladders. Have you ever climbed a spiral staircase? This is what Desi and her friends look like. Each DNA molecule has two strands that fit together to make the ladder, so it is called a DOUBLE HELIX. The DNA strands are made of a bunch of smaller units that repeat over and over. Those DNA UNITS are made of even smaller parts.

A DNA molecule is in the shape of a *double helix*.

Let's take a closer look at Desi's DNA units. Just as you have parts that fit together to make your body, a DNA unit has parts, too. Desi's DNA units have three parts: a sugar, a phosphate, and a base. Let's start with the part that sounds familiar—sugar! The word *sugar* probably makes you think of food—ice cream, candy, Popsicles…yum! The sugar in Desi is the same kind of molecule, and it has a big name…deoxyribose! Desi's sugar is connected to a phosphate group (the second part of a DNA unit). It's called a phosphate because it contains the element phosphorus.

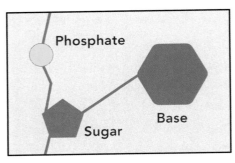

A DNA UNIT is made of three parts.

Walk your fingers along the rungs of the DNA ladder as if you are climbing it.

Strands

Can you find the three parts of a DNA unit? Try to say their names.

DNA molecules have repeating units made of sugar, phosphate, and bases.

Now for the really exciting part! Did you know that DNA has its own alphabet? Our alphabet has 26 letters, but the DNA alphabet only has 4! Those letters are A, T, C, and G. Each of those letters stands for a big word. A is adenine, T is thymine, C is cytosine, and G is guanine. Remember how we learned that each small unit of DNA has three parts? Well, the third part is called the base. The base is either an A, T, C, or G.

DNA also contains a code! Look at Desi and check out her bases (A, T, C, and G). Can you see a pattern? If you noticed that an A on one strand of Desi's DNA always pairs up with a T, you are right! You can also see that a C is always matched up with a G! If you know the DNA alphabet on one side of a DNA strand, you always know the other side, too. Just use the rule! The BASE PAIRING rule is: A always pairs with T, and C always pairs with G. Would you like an easy way to remember this rule? Think of **A**pple **T**rees and **C**hewing **G**um. That's right! A with T, and C with G. You've got it!

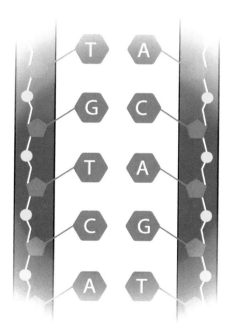

DNA molecules have four kinds of bases: Adenine (A), Thymine (T), Cytosine (C), and Guanine (G).

In DNA, A always pairs with T and C always pairs with G.

Uh-oh. There are some lost **DNA BASES**. *They are sad to be without their partners. Remember, A and T are best buddies, and C and G always hang together. Can you draw lines to match each base up with its base pair buddy?*

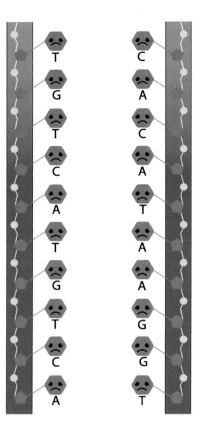

Y̶ou may be wondering why A is always with T, and C is always with G. Well, it turns out that's the only way for a DNA molecule to fit together. It's like a puzzle. Have you ever tried to put a puzzle piece in the wrong spot? No matter how hard you try, it just doesn't fit! Back in the 1950s, scientists were racing to figure out the shape of DNA. Rosalind Franklin used X-rays to take pictures of DNA molecules. Her pictures proved that DNA was shaped like a spiral. Using that new information, two men named James Watson and Francis Crick built a big model of DNA to finally figure out how the pieces fit together. Desi's structure was discovered!

If you could become super tiny and walk along a DNA staircase, the steps would be made of base pairs. The sides of the staircase would be made of sugars and phosphates. All of Desi's parts are held together by chemical bonds.

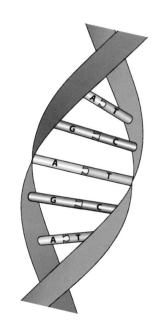

Now you've learned a lot about Desi's parts and how she is put together, but what does she do? Why do you have DNA in every cell of your body? It all goes back to that DNA alphabet. If you are going to bake cookies, you need a recipe. If you are going to put a new toy together, you need instructions. Our bodies are the same! In order to put a living thing together, the instructions written in DNA are needed! The A, T, C, and G of the DNA alphabet carry the information to build other molecules.

Now, think back to the beginning when you looked at your arm. Remember, the skin you see is made up of lots of skin cells, and each one has a nucleus filled with Desi and her DNA friends. Where else in your body can you find DNA? If you said everywhere, you are right! You have muscle cells, bone cells, blood cells, brain cells, stomach cells, and many other cells. Every single cell in your body has the same DNA code in its nucleus. Your DNA is being used all the time to make molecules and keep your cells—and you—alive!

Your cells can read the order of bases in your DNA, just like you read the order of letters in a book.

What about other living things? Would you find Desi the DNA molecule in the cells of a cat? How about a horse's cells? Yes! The exact same kind of DNA molecules, made up of the same DNA alphabet, are found in all living things. Look around your house or out the window. Can you see three different living things? Maybe you see your pet dog, a giant tree in your backyard, a bird flying by, or a tiny weed growing out of a crack in the sidewalk Desi the DNA molecule can be found in all of these living organisms! Pretty cool, right? Now you get the chance to build your own DNA molecule—and eat it, too!

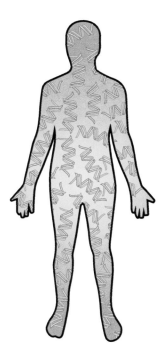

Build Your Own DNA Model

INSTRUCTIONS

Let's learn more about the parts of DNA by building a model. Remember, DNA strands are made of units hooked together. Those DNA units have three parts:

1. sugar
2. phosphate
3. base (A, T, C, or G)

Start with one piece of licorice. This will be one of the sides of your DNA molecule. Remember, it is made of sugar and phosphates. Stick ten toothpicks, spaced evenly, along the length of the licorice piece. Now stick one marshmallow (any color) on each toothpick and slide it on until it nearly touches the licorice. You should still have an empty side of each toothpick sticking out to use in one of the next steps.

Before you go on, you need to make a key for your model. The marshmallows are the four DNA bases: adenine (A), thymine (T), cytosine (C), and guanine (G). You get to decide which color of marshmallow is used for each base. Write down the colors on the lines below.

> ## MATERIALS
>
> - two thick pieces of licorice
> - toothpicks
> - mini marshmallows (four different colors)*

Marshmallow Color	DNA Base
_____	Adenine (A)
_____	Thymine (T)
_____	Cytosine (C)
_____	Guanine (G)

---

* If you don't have marshmallows, you can substitute any kind of soft candy that comes in four different colors. (For a healthier version, you can substitute four types of fruit for the marshmallows. Grapes, chunks of pineapple, and pieces of cherries and strawberries work well.)

Build Your Own DNA Model

INSTRUCTIONS (continued)

Now you're ready to build the other side of your DNA. Remember, each base will pair up with another base. Do you remember the rule? That's right. A always pairs with T, and C always pairs with G. Now you need to choose your marshmallows carefully. If the first marshmallow you put on was an A, you need to put a T marshmallow next to it. If the first one was C, you need to put a G next to it. Go ahead and pair up all ten bases by sliding another marshmallow onto each toothpick.

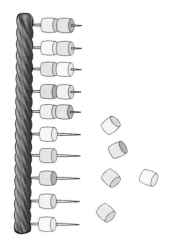

Check your model. What color did you use for A? What color did you use for T? Are your A's paired up with your T's? Check to make sure your C's and G's are paired up, too. Now all you need to do is add the second strand—the other side of your DNA molecule. Do this by taking your second piece of licorice and sliding it onto the toothpicks so it lines up with your first strand.

You should have a licorice, double marshmallow, and licorice sandwich! The toothpicks are the bonds that hold the bases together in the middle. There is one last step. Is DNA like a straight staircase or a twisted one? It's twisted! Carefully hold the top of both licorice strands and the bottom of both strands, and twist them in opposite directions. You have a double helix DNA molecule! The DNA model you built is much larger than actual DNA. Desi and her friends are so small that we can't even see them, but your model has the same shape. Good job! Now you can reward yourself with a little snack. Just don't eat the bonds!

ACTIVITY
2

Base Pairing with Buddies

INSTRUCTIONS

You've made a model of a DNA molecule like Desi, and now you get the chance to be part of one yourself! First, cut out the DNA base cards on page 23 to label yourself and your friends. Choose which base you would like to be—adenine (A), thymine (T), cytosine (C), or guanine (G)—and stick the card to your shirt with tape. Now you need enough friends or stuffed animals to be the other DNA bases. Label each friend with a base card, and you're ready to go!

MATERIALS

- 9 buddies (friends or stuffed animals work great)
- scissors
- 2 pieces of string or yarn (about 5 feet each)
- printed DNA base cards
- tape

Look around the room. You and your nine buddies should each be labeled with a DNA base card for a total of ten DNA bases. Now it's time to build one strand of the DNA molecule. Lay out one length of string on the floor. Choose five buddies to stand or sit along the length of string. Those buddies look lonely, don't they?

12

ACTIVITY
2

Base Pairing with Buddies

INSTRUCTIONS (continued)

It's time to buddy up. Lay the other length of string along the floor, parallel to the first one. This will be the second DNA strand. Now those lonely bases need a partner. How do you know the order to put the bases on the second strand? Do you remember the base pairing rule? (Think **A**pple **T**rees and **C**hewing **G**um.) That's right! Adenine always pairs with thymine, and cytosine always pairs with guanine. Look at the bases already on the string and figure out which one you should pair with. Help the remaining buddies get paired up, too. Ready, set, base pair!

You should have made five base pairs.

How many were C-G base pairs? _____   How many were A-T base pairs? _____

Do you want an extra challenge? Call your mom or dad to help. Tell her or him to read the secret instructions below.

SECRET INSTRUCTIONS

Parents: If your child wants an extra challenge, instruct him or her to close his or her eyes while you switch around a few of the base pair buddies so they are no longer paired correctly. Then instruct your child to "fix" the DNA strand and see how quickly he or she can pair them back up by following the base pairing rule: A with T, and C with G. Your child can mix them up and "fix" them as many times as he or she wants to reinforce the base pairing concept.

Help Watson and Crick

INSTRUCTIONS

Do you like puzzles? Figuring out how the parts of DNA fit together was like putting together a really hard puzzle. Before the shape of Desi and her friends was discovered, it was a big mystery. Remember Watson and Crick? They knew all the parts of DNA, but they didn't know how to put them together. It was like having a box full of puzzle pieces. They figured out that just like a puzzle, the DNA parts all had their own shapes and sizes, and there was only one way they could fit together. The puzzle was solved when they came up with a double helix structure. The sugar and phosphates fit perfectly along each side with the bases paired up in the middle.

MATERIALS

- DNA unit paper parts
- scissors
- tape

Pretend you are a biologist working back in the year 1953. The structure of Desi and her DNA friends is still unknown. You and other scientists are racing to be the first to solve the puzzle. You know what the smaller pieces are that make up DNA, but you DON'T know how the pieces fit together. Read on for some hints to help you figure this out!

Now, cut out the **DNA pieces on pages 25 and 27 only** and try to put them together. It's tricky! Use the hints below to help you go step-by-step.

HINT 1: Remember, a long DNA molecule with two strands is made of smaller units. Those units are made up of a sugar, a phosphate, and a base (A, T, C, or G). Try building one DNA unit.

Which part of the DNA unit attaches to the base? _____

If you said sugar, you are correct. Only the sugar fits with an A, T, C, or G.

Does your DNA unit look like the one below? Great! Now use the rest of the pieces on **pages 25 and 27** to build four more DNA units.

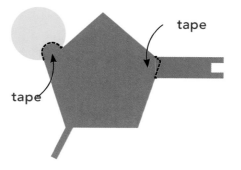

Help Watson and Crick

INSTRUCTIONS (continued)

HINT 2: Now that you have made all of your DNA units for one strand, you are ready to start putting them together. Remember, sugars and phosphates make up the outside of a DNA molecule. They alternate: sugar, phosphate, sugar, phosphate, sugar, _____ . Do you see the pattern?

Let's put one side of the DNA molecule together this way. Use tape to attach the sugar of your first DNA unit to the phosphate of your second DNA unit, and so on, until you have built a chain that is five DNA units long.

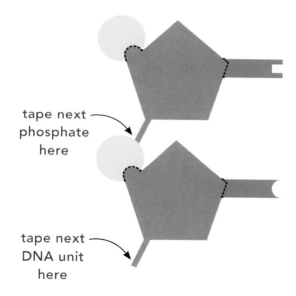

tape next phosphate here

tape next DNA unit here

Good job! You have built one side of the DNA molecule.

Now, cut out the **DNA pieces on pages 29 and 31**. Use the hints below to finish your DNA molecule.

HINT 3: How many strands does a DNA molecule have? Two! Use the pieces from **pages 29 and 31** to make five more DNA units. Remember: hook a sugar, a phosphate, and a base together. You will use these to build the second strand.

Help Watson and Crick

INSTRUCTIONS (continued)

HINT 4: Now you should have five DNA units built. It is time for some base pairing! Remember the rule? Pair A with T and C with G. You will notice that in order to make all the pieces fit, your second strand needs to be upside down. Check it out!

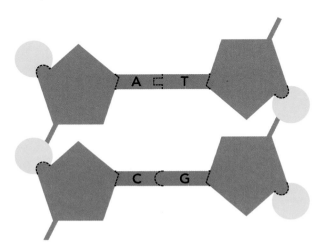

GREAT WORK! You just learned something new about Desi the DNA molecule. Her two DNA strands are pointed in opposite directions! Now you just need some tape to hold it together. Remember, the tape you use is like the bonds found in Desi. You just solved one of the trickiest puzzles in science!

ACTIVITY 4

See DNA for Yourself!

Now that you have learned a lot about Desi and her DNA friends, it's time to see DNA for yourself. You are going to do a DNA EXTRACTION from a living thing. Sound scary? Not really. *Extract* just means *remove*. You are going to separate the DNA from the other stuff inside a cell and take a look at it. Where can you get DNA to extract? If you said from any living thing, you're right! Your mom's favorite flowers have DNA, but that might get you in trouble. Your big toe has DNA—ouch! Let's extract DNA from a fruit or vegetable instead. They contain DNA, just as you do.

MATERIALS

- blender or sealable plastic baggie
- source of DNA*
- measuring spoons
- table salt
- water
- liquid dish detergent
- clear plastic or glass cups
- coffee filter and/or small strainer
- ice-cold rubbing alcohol (put this on ice to cool it down before you begin)
- Popsicle stick or plastic coffee stirrer

INSTRUCTIONS

1. Combine your DNA source, 1/8 tsp. salt, and 1 cup of cold water in a blender. Blend on high for about 15 seconds. (If you don't have a blender, you can instead mash up these ingredients well inside a sealed plastic bag.) When your mixture is like chunky soup, you're ready for the next step.

   What's happening? You're crushing your DNA source to help release the DNA from the cells. The salt helps create a good environment for the DNA to separate and be seen.

2. Pour your soupy cell mixture through a small strainer and collect the liquid in another container. (You can also use a coffee filter, but you'll need to first place the filter in the container and tape it over the outside edge to hold it in place.) Wait for all of the liquid to come through the filter. The material left over on top of the filter can be thrown away.

   What's happening? You threw away the cell leftovers and other things you don't need that were too large to make it through the filter. The DNA is in the liquid you collected.

---

* DNA sources: Try this procedure with strawberries, peas, spinach, broccoli, or a banana. (Just choose one and use about 1/2 cup. Fresh materials are great. If you are using frozen food, thaw it to room temperature before beginning.)

See DNA for Yourself!

INSTRUCTIONS (continued)

3. Add two tablespoons of liquid dish detergent to the liquid you collected and swirl to mix. Avoid making lots of bubbles and allow this mixture to sit for 5–10 minutes. Now divide the soapy mixture into several plastic cups or other small glass containers. (The containers must be clear so you can see through them!)

What's happening? The soap helps to further break down the cells and release the DNA.

4. Pour ice-cold alcohol carefully down the side of your cup until you have added about the same amount of alcohol as the soapy mixture already in the cup. Pour the alcohol slowly and carefully so it settles in a nice layer on top. (Using an eyedropper to add the alcohol slowly is helpful.) Repeat this for each cup. Let your cups sit undisturbed for a few minutes.

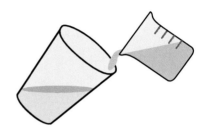

What's happening? DNA does not dissolve in alcohol. The alcohol and the cold temperature make it difficult for DNA to stay mixed. Right now, the DNA is coming out of the solution, so you will be able to see it.

5. Carefully hold the cup up at eye level. Look for white clumps where the alcohol layer meets the soapy mixture. Do you see stringy stuff? That's DNA! You can collect it by slowly swirling your wooden stick or plastic coffee stirrer around that layer. If you want to save it, transfer it to another container filled with alcohol.

What's happening? You just extracted DNA. That white stuff you see is made up of Desi and her friends. How come you can't see the double helix shape? Well, because the DNA you just extracted is made up of lots and lots of DNA molecules. The double helix shape of just one DNA molecule is too small to see.

Great job! You may have heard that scientists can use DNA to figure out who committed a crime or why someone is sick. The very first step in any DNA investigation is to extract DNA. You just did that. Congratulations!

Curiosity Connector

Here are some links to help you follow your curiosity!

- Watch an animated tutorial called "What is DNA?"
  http://learn.genetics.utah.edu/content/molecules/dna/

- Practice base pairing with an interactive website.
  http://learn.genetics.utah.edu/content/molecules/builddna/

- Click through the first section of this animation to learn more about how Watson and Crick discovered the puzzle of DNA structure.
  http://www.dnaftb.org/19/animation.html

- Make an origami DNA molecule!
  http://www.dnacenter.com/science-technology/dna-education/dna-origami.html

- Read this for a review of DNA structure with diagrams.
  http://www.ducksters.com/science/biology/dna.php

Activity 4 Sources:

- NOVA Science NOW: Extracting DNA from Bananas
  http://www-tc.pbs.org/wgbh/nova/education/activities/pdf/3214_01_nsn_01.pdf

- How to Extract DNA from a Strawberry
  http://www.genome.gov/pages/education/modules/strawberryextractioninstructions.pdf

- Genetic Science Learning Center: How to Extract DNA from Anything Living
  http://learn.genetics.utah.edu/content/labs/extraction/howto/

What are you CURIOUS about?

Glossary

BASE PAIRING – the specific pairing of bases in a DNA molecule: adenine with thymine and cytosine with guanine

DNA – deoxyribonucleic acid; the genetic material in your cells

DNA BASES – the DNA alphabet: adenine, thymine, cytosine, and guanine

DNA EXTRACTION – the process of removing DNA from its source

DNA UNIT – sugar, phosphate, and base; the parts that make up a DNA molecule

DOUBLE HELIX – the spiral shape of a two-stranded DNA molecule

NUCLEUS – the center of a cell, where DNA is located

Tools for Your Tool Kit

Let's make the ideas you learned today part of your life tool kit. Remember to print out some blank tool kit pages and tape or glue on today's tools.

1. DNA molecules are shaped like a _____ .

   Add **DOUBLE HELIX** to your tool kit!

2. What are the three parts of a DNA unit?

   _____ , _____ , _____

   Add **DNA UNIT** to your tool kit!

3. Which base always pairs with adenine? _____

   Which base always pairs with cytosine? _____

   Add **BASE PAIRING** to your tool kit!

4. Which of the following could DNA be extracted from? _____

   fern, moth, fish, rock, moss, magnet

   Add **DNA EXTRACTION** to your tool kit!

A (adenine)	**G** (guanine)
A (adenine)	**G** (guanine)
C (cytosine)	**G** (guanine)
C (cytosine)	**T** (thymine)
C (cytosine)	**T** (thymine)

Cutouts for Activity 3: Help Watson and Crick

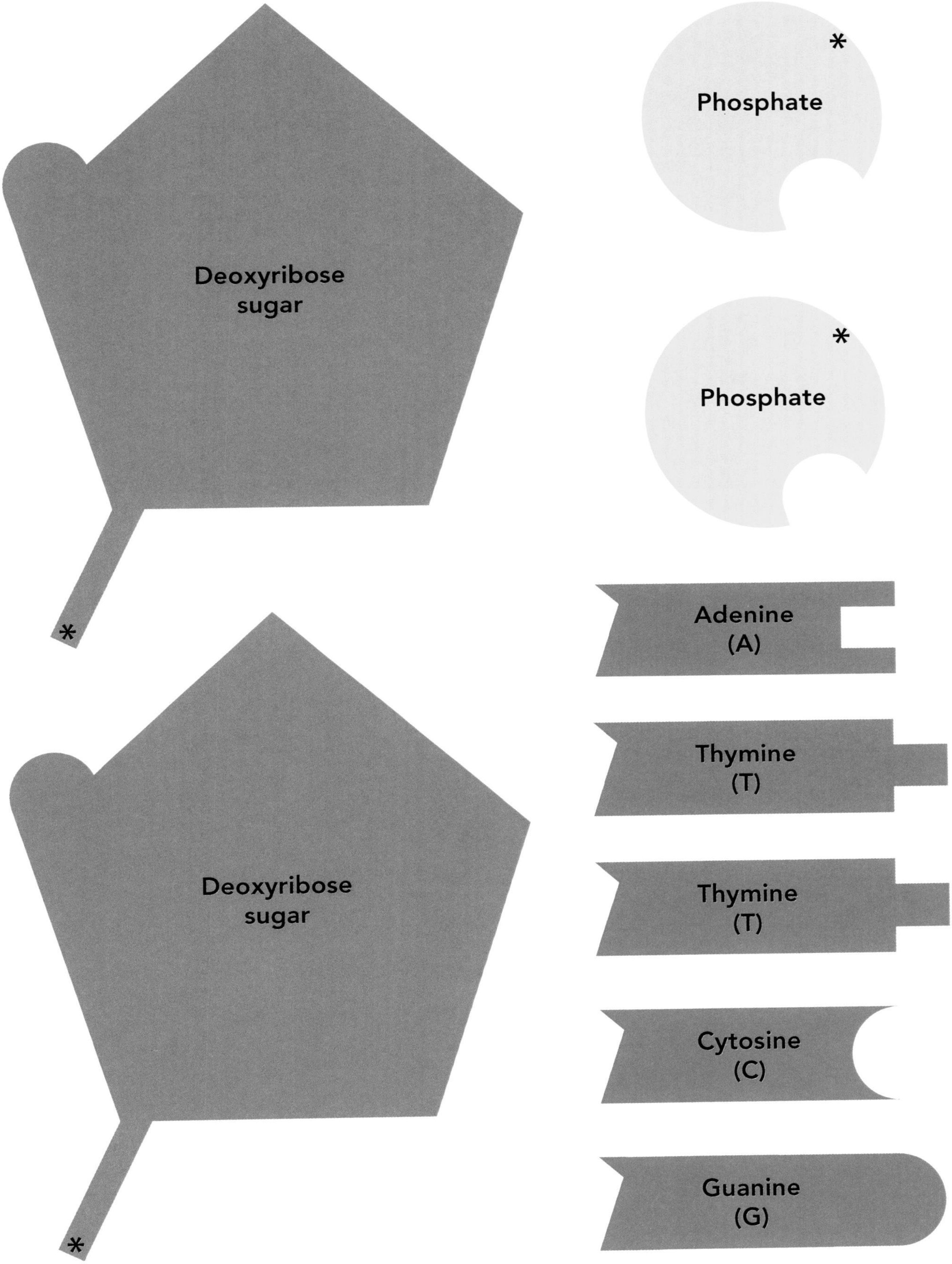

Deoxyribose sugar
*
Deoxyribose sugar
*
Phosphate
*
Phosphate
*
Adenine (A)
Thymine (T)
Thymine (T)
Cytosine (C)
Guanine (G)

Cutouts for Activity 3: Help Watson and Crick

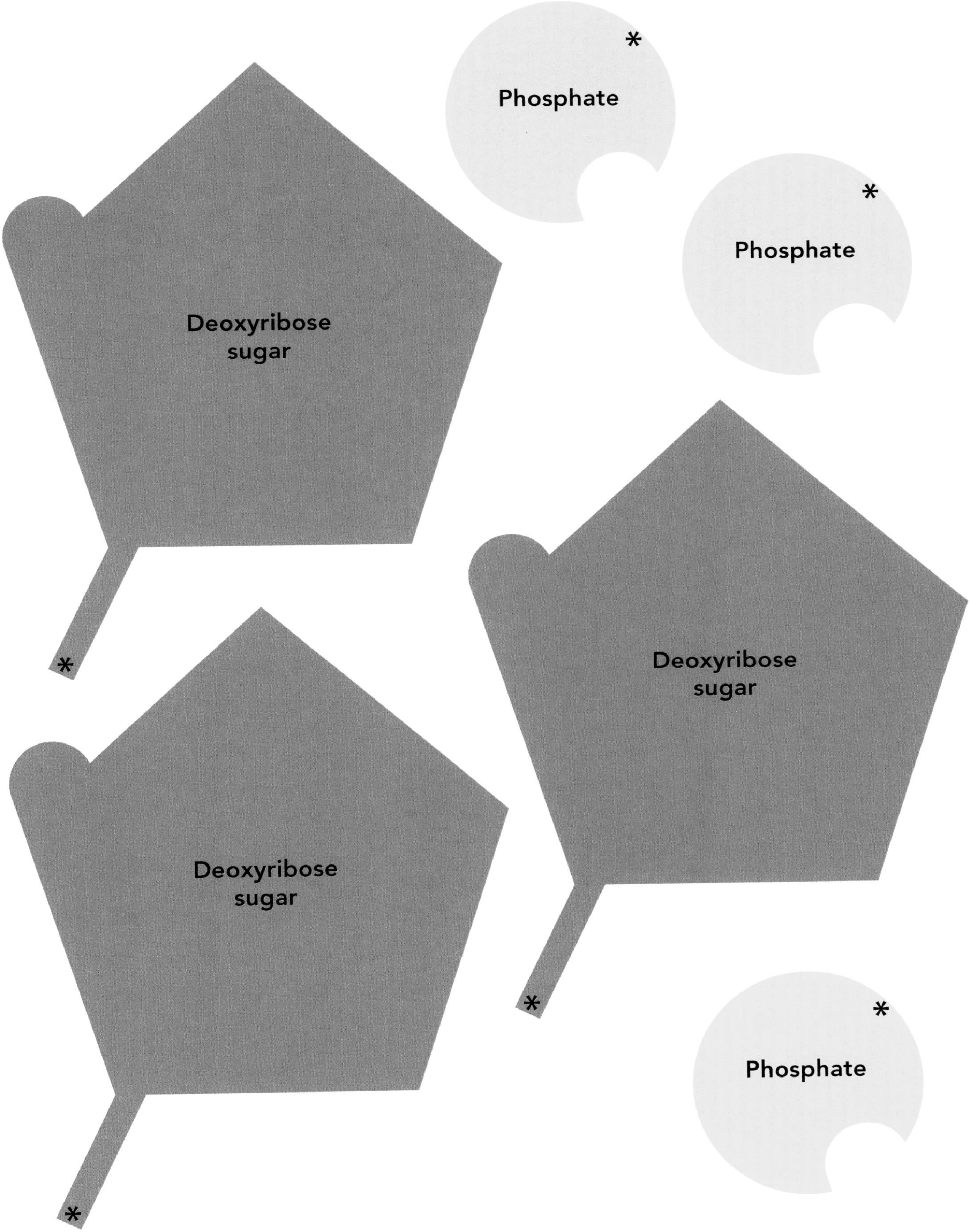

Phosphate
*
Phosphate
*
Deoxyribose sugar
*
Deoxyribose sugar
*
Deoxyribose sugar
*
Phosphate
*

Cutouts for Activity 3: Help Watson and Crick

*
Deoxyribose sugar
Phosphate
*
Phosphate
*
*
Deoxyribose sugar
Adenine (A)
Adenine (A)
Thymine (T)
Cytosine (C)
Guanine (G)

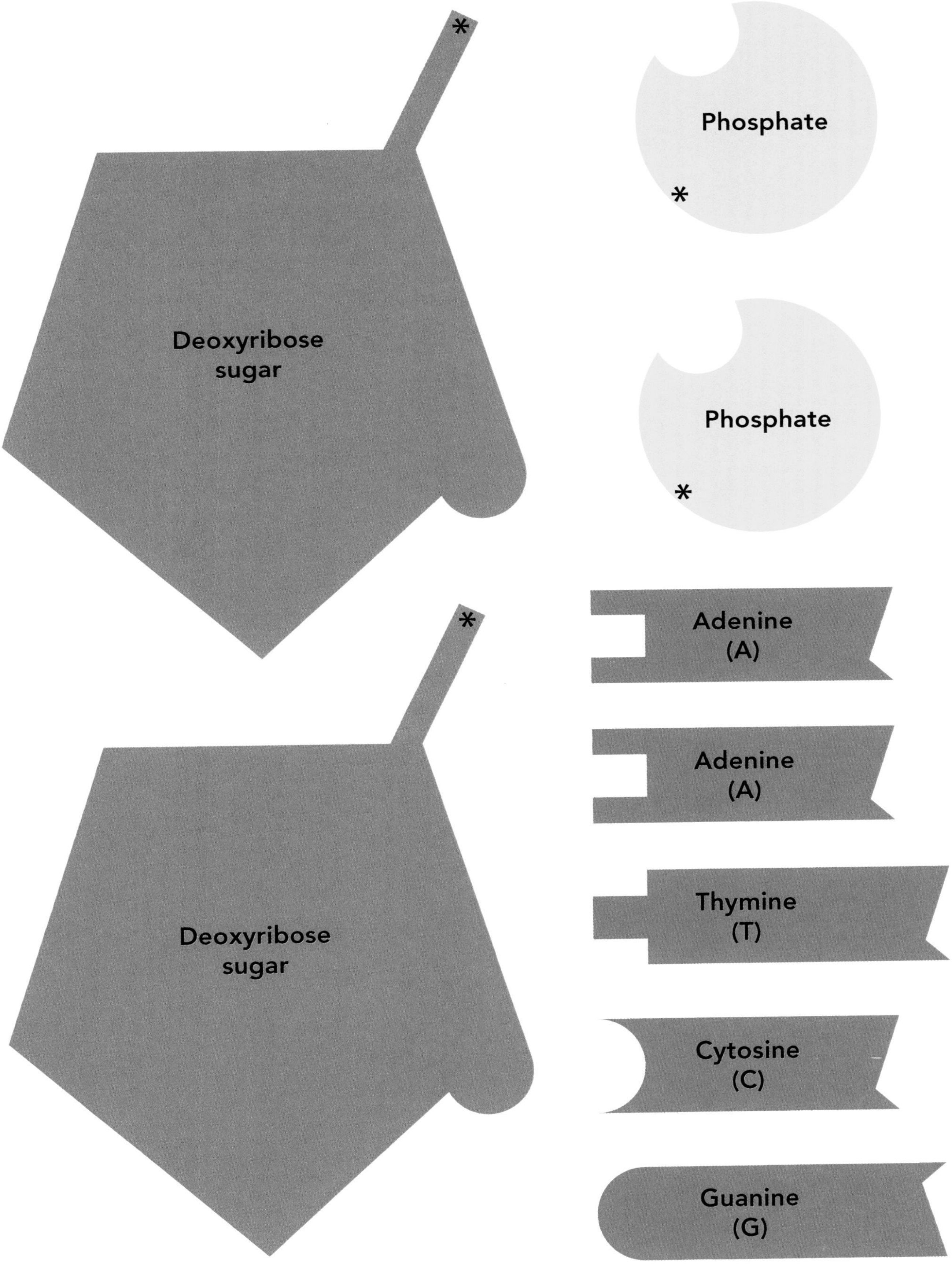

*

Phosphate

*

Deoxyribose
sugar

Phosphate

*

*

*

Deoxyribose
sugar

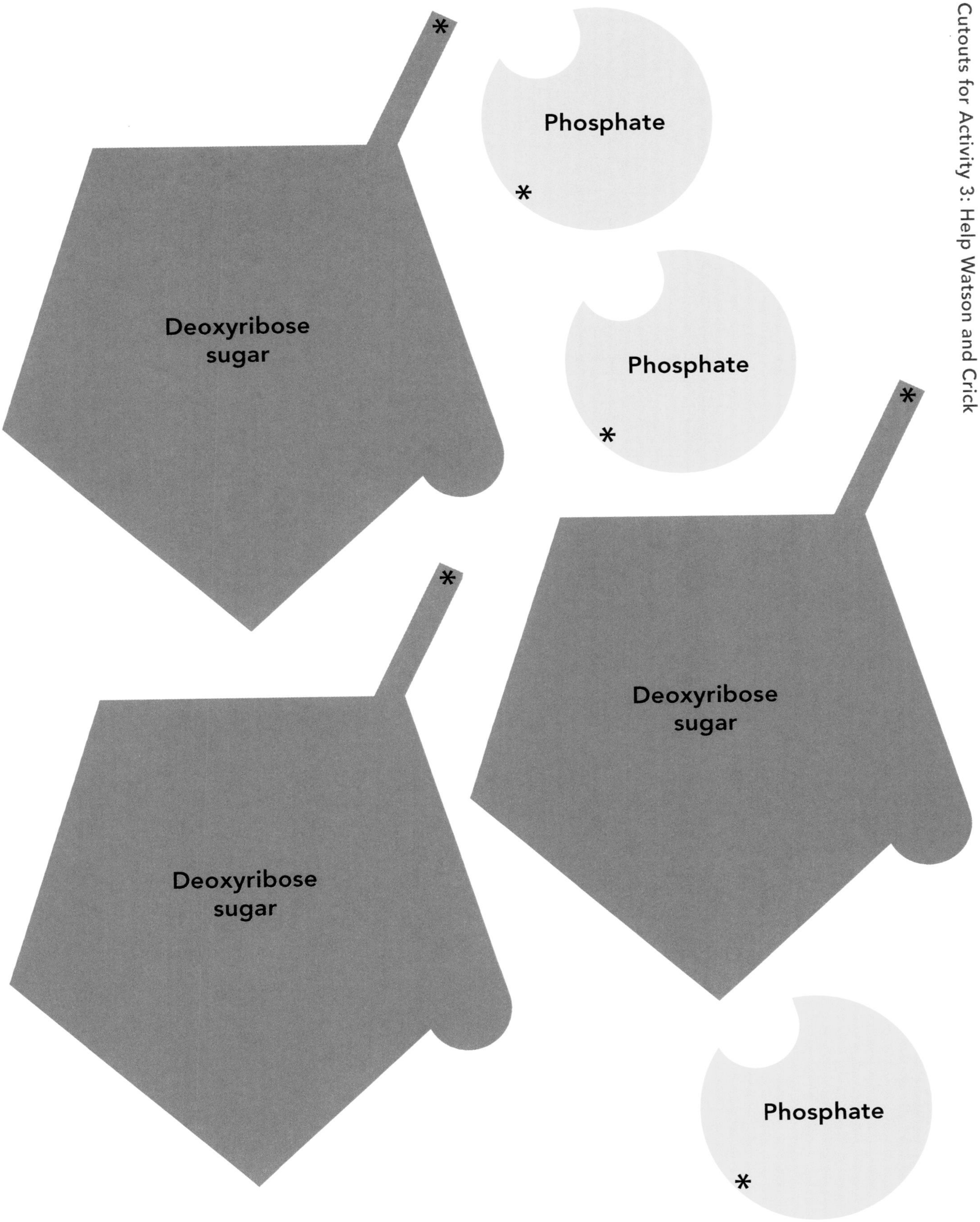

Deoxyribose
sugar

Phosphate

*

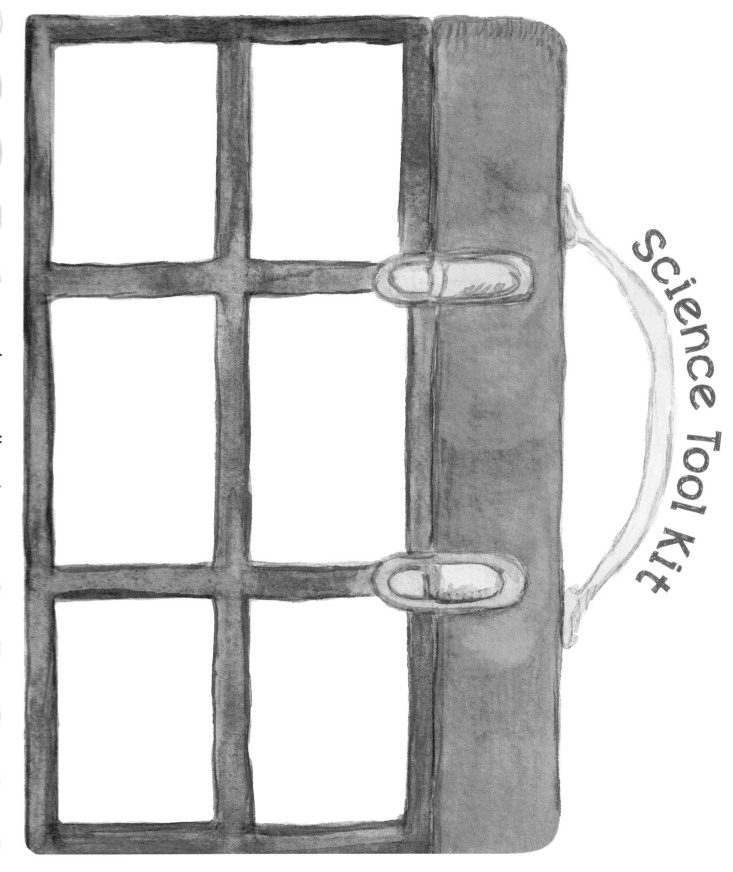

Science Tool Kit

Made in the USA
Middletown, DE
02 November 2020